A Year in C

By Jacob

In the small town of Rogers, young couple. They lived in a small two bedroom, two bathrooms home. The home was small but it was enough for the young couple who had just gotten married last month. The month of October had come upon this small town and the weather was starting to get cooler and it was raining much more often now.

The youngest one of the couple was George. He was 30 years old and had pale brown hair. He was of rather tall height being six feet tall. He had brown eyes that pretty much matched up with his brown hair. He was skinny having lost 50 pounds in the past year so he could fit into his suit for the wedding. His wife, Laura, was two years older and had very beautiful light blonde hair. She was shorter and only five feet and eight inches tall. She had a very nice looking pair of blue eyes. Since she was such a natural beautiful skinny person; this motivated George to lose his excess weight so he could match her better.

It was a warm summerlike day in the middle of September when they had their wedding. It was an outdoor wedding because they wanted to take advantage of these last nice days for the year. The wedding went along well enough except for one minor incident. The best man of the wedding was George's brother, Luke. Luke showed up for the wedding on time and did everything he was supposed to but when he was giving the toast some very rude comments were made. He accused George of taking Laura away from him when he knew well enough that he had no chance with Laura. At the time most people just thought he was under the influence of alcohol but these statements were confirmed by him the next week when he was over at their house. This lead to a splitting up of the two to the point where they have not spoken to each up to this point in time, a month later.

Now the couple was the church going type of people. It was a bright, sunny Sunday morning when they decided they would go out to church. "I do hope they have communion today" said Laura. "I agree" said George. Once they arrived at church, it was about a ten minute drive through the country roads" they noticed that there was a more than normal amount of cars in the parking lot. "I wonder why all of these people are here today" said George. "I don't know but something must be going on" Laura said. They both got out of their car and walked into the church together, holding hands like they always do. Upon walking into the church they noticed the large amount of people in the area. "Wow, I have never seen this many people in this particular church in my life before" George said. "Me neither, I think something important must be going on today. Maybe there is a special speaker that is going to speak today" said Laura. "Just maybe there might be" said George.

Now they proceeded to find their normal seat in the pew and sat down just like it was any other Sunday in the church. The pastor of the church was a Reverend Doug Myers. However, most people usually referred to him as just Pastor Doug. Now, Pastor Doug was a calm nice older man that was nearing retirement age. He was a shorter stockier person with a bald head and gray hair on only the sides. He started late in his career of ministry and just became a pastor for the United Methodist church when he was in his fifties. Having had a previous career of marketing, he left the business world to pursue his calling to ministry. One of his favorite lines he always says is that he did not leave the business world to go into ministry for the money. No, he did it because he felt that was what God was leading him to do.

Upon walking up to the front of the church, Pastor Doug greeted the congregation in his normal jubilant way and proceeded to tell of the announcements for the week. "There is a Trustee meeting this Monday, and as always we have our Kid's Club and Adult Bible Study on Tuesday night." He said. "But the most important announcement yet that I have to give to you is that there will be a special guest speaker for the message today. It is my great honor to introduce the bishop for the Eastern Ohio United Methodist Conference, Bishop Bickerton. Now this will be his final year here in this conference and he wanted to visit all of the churches in the conference in his last year and speak personally to each one of them. Now what he mostly wants to talk about is his commitment to missions and ministry even after his retirement. Now, I have decided to forgo the normal routine on Sunday morning to allow him to have more time to speak. So let us collect the offering for today and then the Bishop can proceed to talk."

So the offering was collected for the day and then the Bishop proceeded to make his way to the front of the church. Now the Bishop was a very tall man that was actually around Pastor Doug's age. However he had much more time in ministry than the Pastor did. He had been on many mission trips in his lifetime. He went to Africa, many countries in Latin America, Europe, and Israel or the Holy Land. He was a very accomplished man that was now nearing his last few months of work and was looking forward to his many years of retirement. Now the Bishop had made his way to the pulpit and began to speak.

"It is with great honor to be assembled before you here today" he said. "I would like to speak about the many great mission opportunities that there are in both local and international areas. Everybody has their own purpose in life and also has an area of mission that they are called to in life. I have been around many countries and have seen many things. I have seen poverty, starvation, and racial cruelty, not to mention many other unjust things. I have to say that as much as I try minimal improvement has happened in those areas. I have helped to put together buildings; I have taught the local children about the bible and religion, most important of all I have provided food and supplies to the locals and the poor communities of the area."

"I would like to talk about the impact that each of these three things have in the community. First are the housing projects I have assisted in. I have helped to drywall, assembled house siding, and even installed plumbing and electrical wiring. These things help and I believe that it gives some families a new home to live in. But the main problem with these things is that once the housing project is complete what are we left with? We built a few houses and gave a few families a place to live in but then we leave never to come back again. Yes it looks good on us. We take pictures of the house; we show the smiles of the volunteers helping and the jubilant smiles of the family moving into the finished house. Then we go back to our home church in the states and show these lovely pictures to congregation and we say we built three houses and now three families that were homeless now have a place to live in. But out of the thousands of people and families that were homeless we now have but helped just three of those families. How do we solve this problem? What kind of projects do we need to implement to keep these construction projects going? What will it take? Go ahead and talk amongst yourselves for the next five minutes on what you think can be done about this problem. I will be around to check in on these conversations."

Everyone seemed to be taken off guard at this request. They had never been asked to talk out questions like this before. However, after a few seconds of awkward silence they began to talk this question out. Many people believed that the best route was to have people hired that lived in these countries. Their job description would be to build these houses. This proposal was quickly criticized because it presented a new set of problems. How do you decide who gets the job in these countries to build these houses? Also of issue was where you can get the funds to pay these people. So the general consensus that most people came to is that you have to have volunteer workers to do the job. "Now let's come back together and discuss our results from this conversation" the Bishop said. Everybody came back together and once everything had quieted down the Bishop began to speak again. "I was walking around and this is mostly what I heard people talking about." he said. "I heard people discussing that we would need a permanent volunteer force that lived in these countries year around. This is mostly what I came to a conclusion of before I came here today. However there is still the problem of finding these people to do the project. It is defiantly something that needs to be improved upon"

"Now the second thing I would like to discuss is the teaching of religion that I participated in while I was on these mission trips" the Bishop said. "It is crucial that we not only help the poor by building houses and providing food but by also sharing a little about our faith with them. I believe that this part is one of the most overlooked aspects of a mission trip. Sure it is important to provide thing like food and shelter, but it is also important to teach them about our faith and about God. On a recent trip to Africa I decided to take a large amount of time and devote it to teaching the bible to the locals. I taught them about the bible stories and shared with them some of the greatest stories that I believe most people should know from the bible. Now most people here in this congregation have probably heard of Noah, or David and Goliath since they were kids. Growing up around bible stories is what most children of the past generation did. But today the table has turned. Most children today even in this country do not know of these stories. They do not grow up with their parents reading these stories. Actually, some homes probably do not even have a Bible. But in Africa few people even know how to read. Taking this fact into account I decided to change that. I decided to read these stories to the people on my last mission trip. It went over well. With the help of a local translator the stories were easily translated into their own native language. I received many thanks from them and much praise for taking my time to read these stories. I believed it made a huge impact on their lives. I made them think about Jesus and their own lives in contrast to the teachings of the bible. I might have even brought some people to drastically think about changing their lives around. But then I left. I would probably never come back to the area to see these people again. I planted the seed in them, but there was nothing to continue to nurture this seed and make it grow. There were no local United Methodist churches, or to even broaden the perspective there was no local churches that were of the Christian faith that were not ten or more miles away. Now these people living in this remote village had no cars or other method of transportation besides horses. But even with horses there were no well built roads to travel this distance. So I was left at a kind of standstill on what to do there.

So now I move on to my third and last item of discussion with you today. While on this mission trip I distributed food and helped to cook many meals for the local people in this village. I learned upon arriving that about one year ago about 10% of the population of the village lost their lives due to starvation in a famine. Many of the most respected elders are the ones who lost their lives. They were the oldest and weakest to begin with but in this African culture the oldest are the most respected because they are believed to know the most and be the wisest of the village. The reason for the famine was that the crops were bad that year due to a severe drought in the area. Now I helped to bring some relief to a region that was just recovering from this famine. The crops were better this year and the food stores replenished somewhat. When I went I added much more food to the stores and cooked many meals with the help of my friends for the local people. But then just like before in the last problem, I left. So the same type of problem arises. Who would continue to provide food for these people in this village? They can usually provide food for themselves but what if they have another drought again like last year? So at this problem most people, including me, are at a standstill.

So you are probably wondering why I have decided to tell you this long and very detailed story. Why you might ask would I spend each of my Sunday mornings visiting the local United Methodist churches and giving this same speech. Well the simple answer is to challenge you. I want you to take it upon yourself to put yourself into a mission field of your own. You might say I am too busy. Well I can tell you about the many opportunities that require little time but make a big impact in the community. You might say I don't like to travel. Well there are many things you can do just in this area to make an impact. You don't have to go to big places far away and do something. You can stay in your own local community and still make a big impact. I am nearing retirement age; I don't have the energy to continue this forever. So I need younger people to rise up to this challenge and help out. Don't forget to take a friend along for the journey. Thank you for taking the time to listen and have a blessed day"

The Bishop had finished speaking and the service had come to a close. Everybody began to rise from their sits and started to make their way out of the church. On their way out of the church George and Laura shook hands with the bishop and thanked them for his wonderful speech and for taking the time to visit. Then they began to make their way to their car. Once in the car and heading down the road they began to discuss what they had heard. Laura was the first to speak. "So what did you think of the speech today?" she said. "Well, I thought it was a very good speech" he said. "I think that we need to think about what we can do to help out in the community. You know there are a lot of people right around here that need our help." I agree" said Laura. "But don't you think it would be nice to visit a foreign country and help out there? I mean we can help out locally but I would like to take a step out in faith and go somewhere different." Hearing this kind of made George uneasy because he had never been out of the country in his life. Laura on the other hand had visited many countries in her young life. She travelled for business to many countries in Europe not to mention Canada and Australia. So the thought to visit a new country kind of came as a natural thing to her. "I don't know if I would want to spend time away from home in a foreign country" said George. "It kind of makes me uneasy to go to another country where I don't know the language or the culture." But that's what makes it exciting and interesting" said Laura. "Why don't you pray and think on it this week and maybe next weekend we can have a good idea on what we want to do." That sounds good" he said. "I will go for that. Give me some time and I will let you know what conclusion I have reached and you can let me know what conclusion you have reached."

"Agreed," said Laura. "I think that's a good idea for the both of us."

So they both thought about it long and hard over the next week.

Laura started looking online to find countries that she had never visited before. She had been to many countries in Europe and felt comfortable there on her business trips. Laura was the CEO of an investment firm based out of nearby Pittsburgh, PA. She had made her way very far up the corporate ladder considering her young age. She was talented in the business world. Having done well in math in high school she decided to go to college to major in Business Administration. Having graduated in the top 10 of her class she proceeded to attend the prestigious college of Princeton University and she attained a master's degree in Business Administration after only six years of schooling. Now she decided that although she was comfortable in those European countries she thought she would try a different part of the globe, a different continent that offered diverse challenges and was in need of help. Although she had been to many countries she had never participated in any kind of religious or missionary work outside of her own country. Many of her overseas trips involved sitting in rather boring business meetings and deciding what should be done about the investment firm's local business in this country. She never really had much of a chance to explore the area and find out what the culture was like. Most of her impressions on what the countries culture was like came from the people she met with that were from that country. Having enjoyed her job but wanting to take time off for missionary work she decided that she would like to take a whole year to visit another country and participate in mission opportunities.

So what she started to do is she looked on the computer for local mission opportunities in different countries. She started to look more closely into the Latin American Countries. She went through Guatemala, El Salvador, Mexico, and finally Costa Rica. Upon looking at Costa Rica she noticed that there was a great need for help in the area of Heredia. The country of Costa Rica is divided into what is known as provinces. The province of Heredia is located about mid center of the country just north of the capital city of San Jose. She noticed that two school teachers were needed in this province of Heredia to teach local school children for one year at a local Christian school. At first when she saw this she was very excited and immediately thought this was the right one. However after she really thought this was the opportunity they needed worries and nervousness started to creep into her mind. She saw that it would be one year and thought that maybe that would be too long. She also thought that she was no teacher and maybe was not cut out to teach local children. Her third fear was the language barrier. Sure she took Spanish in high school but she could not remember all of that anymore. And on top of all that was the fact that her husband would probably not want to go along with this plan. She found out about this on Monday and decided that she would continue to pray about it over the upcoming week and tell her husband about it on Saturday. Then she thought that maybe after a long discussion he would be more open to this big change and opportunity for the two of them. Hopefully he would go along with her thoughts and they could undertake this exciting challenge together.

Now George went along a different path in the following week than Laura did. He really did not give it much thought. He thought that it would be great to do something in the local community. However, never being out of the country meant that he was a little leery of travelling to a foreign country. But, he knew that if his wife was with him on the trip that he would do okay. He also knew that he needed to step out of his comfort zone and do something different in life. But his thought into what country he wanted to travel to was minimal. He figured that Laura had already looked into it and had a great idea of where to go so he spend very little time trying to find his own destination. The little time he had spent was when he went onto the computer and decided to do a short search on international missions. He saw the problems in Africa and thought that maybe he could help out there. But the thoughts of malaria and other insects and diseases deterred him from seriously considering this route. So he decided to wait for Laura's response on what she thought. Now George worked at a local UPS center. Having graduated High School and not going onto college George was what you would consider to be of average intelligence. He did well in High School and got good grades but his decision to not go to College was probably what hurt him in life. He always said that he could have gone on to college but decided not to and ended up getting a decent paying job delivering packages. His goal in life was not to be high achieving like Laura but to be more average and do something that he liked to do. However his religious faith is what gave him the kind heart and caring personality that kept him involved in the community.

Now that the weekend had arrived George and Laura decided to sit down at the table and discuss their week and what they had decided on for a mission opportunity. Laura was the first to speak. "I have given it much thought and have spent much time trying to find what would be right for the both of us" she said. "I looked internationally and saw the country of Costa Rica to be our most suitable opportunity. It is a country that is poorer than us; many people live in rather poorly built homes, and the need for us to preach to them the God's Word is great. I wanted to spend a year in the Heredia Provence down there. There is a local church down there that we could spend our time in and they would be able to provide housing and many mission opportunities for us. They always go out into the community and provide food and play games with the children that end up relating to a bible story that is discussed after the game. I think it is a great opportunity and something that we should seriously consider about doing. So, what have you decided about what we should do?" "Well, I really don't know" George said. "I was looking at a country down in Africa that I thought might be an interesting opportunity. But then I saw all of the diseases down there that you can contract and I thought that might not be the best place to go. How are the local diseases in Costa Rica? "Well, I had the same concern as you did at first" Laura spoke. "But then I became more reassured that Costa Rica does not have all of these diseases. My main fear about going into Africa was about these diseases also. I want to be able to enjoy myself on a mission trip without having to worry about contracting some possibly fatal disease. So to answer your question in short, yes I believe that Costa Rica would be a safe country for us to travel to." "That's good" said George. "You know what I think it would be good for us to get away for a year and see another country. After all we have the funds available and work can wait. I think this would open up our eyes to the reality of a different culture. It would give us more respect for people of a different culture and race. It would also make it easier for us to learn the Spanish language. "I agree" said Laura. "I think we should look into the possibilities for us to go there. I know there is a group leaving to go there in the middle of January. I know it might be short notice but I think we could leave then and return in mid January the next year. What do you say?" "I agree to that" said George. "I would be willing to leave then. After all, it would be the middle of the winter and Costa Rica will obviously be much warmer since it is so close to the equator" George said jokingly.

So it was decided, they would be going to Costa Rica. On such short notice and with little time left until the middle of January, Laura had to jump into the planning. In fact the following day she had already called down there and announced and explained to them she and her husband's willingness to go on this year long tip. They were delighted to hear of these plans and their willingness to serve the Lord. They said that it would be short notice but they would be more than willing to accompany them into their schedule. So with that taken care of Laura booked the airplane tickets for the two of them on the date of January 15. Having already both previously gotten their passport, George already having one but never using it before, they were both ready for this relatively large trip involving the both of them being away from home for the next year. They told Pastor Doug about their trip. Having been so delighted to hear of their willingness to do this he thought it would be great to let them share of their adventures upon their return. So everything was in place and it became an anxious period of waiting for January 15.

During this period of waiting there were no shortages of things to do however. They had a bible study to do together in the month preceding their departure and they had many other little tasks to take care of so things would be in place back home when they are gone for the year. This was an exciting time of anticipation for the both of them. George resigned from his job for the year, knowing he would have to find a new job when he returned home. Laura was able to still be a part in her company. She would be able to do some tasks from Costa Rica to still run her company that she was CEO of. However she did appoint an acting CEO to take care of many of the tasks that would need to be done while she was away. She knew that she might be able to spend an hour or two on tasks for her company but most of her time would need to be devoted to the mission trip and helping out down there. So as January 15 started to draw nearer and nearer and the couple started to pack up their things to go on the trip they thought about how to pack for such a large and long length trip. George just packed the necessities but Laura being as women commonly are packed much more than George did. So the morning of January 15 had dawned and both had just woken up early on the morning at 3:00 AM to leave for the Pittsburgh airport.

"Are you ready yet?" called out George to Laura as he was packing the bags into their car. "I think so" said Laura. "I just don't want to forget anything important that we might need. We are going to be gone for a whole year. Anything that we leave behind that we might need is something we will have to purchase down there. I just want to make sure. Are you sure that you have everything George?" "Yes, I think so" George said in a kind of tired mood. Having woken up at 3:00 AM they were both in a very tired state of mind. After both had made a final sweep of the house to make sure nothing was forgotten and everything was put away for the time they were to be gone, they got into the car and departed to the airport. Having both been tired and not wanting to drive they decided to flip a coin to decide who would be driving. It was soon determined that George had won the coin flip leaving Laura to drive. However on the drive there they started to wake up more as the idea of going on this trip made them feel more awake and refreshed. They started to discuss their expectations of the trip.

"So what do you think the accommodations will be like?" asked George to Laura. "Well, I know that we will be living with a family that is within walking distance of the church so whatever they offer us is what we will have. But I am assured that it will be enough and that we will become quite comfortable in the ensuing year" Laura said to George. "Well, that's good as long as I don't have to sleep on the floor for a year" George said jokingly to Laura. They were both laughing at this joke when they read the sign that said the airport was only one mile ahead. "Almost there" said George. "Yes, just about" said Laura. They both pulled into the parking lot in a somewhat tired but also excited mood. Their car would remain there until a friend came along later in the day to pick it up and park it in his driveway so they would not have to pay to park their car for the whole year. It was also a much safer option in his driveway since no one would try to break into it like what might happen in the airport parking lot. So having parked their car and unloaded their bags, they waited at the bus stop that would take them the rest of the way into the airport. The bus came and as they got on it they noticed quite a large amount of people as is normal at this time of the morning. They got to the terminal and both got off of the bus and walked into the terminal with their bags. They checked in with the gate agent, had their passports scanned, checked in their bags, and got their boarding passes. Since there was no direct flight they would first have to fly to Houston and then from Houston on to their final destination of San Jose, Costa Rica. From the San Jose airport they would be picked up by the Pastor of the church and taken to their home where there would be able to unpack and get ready for their welcoming party and dinner this evening. So what happened next I will describe very quickly. They went through security and sat down to wait for their first flight out. They left and arrived in Houston with no problems. They waited for their flight to San Jose and left on time with that. Finally they arrived in San Jose, Costa Rica at 2:30 PM after about a total of six hours flight time. George made a remark about how amazing it was how you could travel 2,700 miles in six hours and even Laura was amazed at how smoothly the whole process seemed to go.

So now that they arrived in Costa Rica safely they proceeded to go through customs. After that they went on to get their bags and began to wait for the person that would pick them up. Upon proceeding to the exit they noticed the large amount of people outside holding signs and telling people who they were waiting for. After looking around for a little while they noticed a person holding a sign with their last names. So they went up to the guy and he noticed who they were immediately. Apparently he had seen a picture of them prior to leaving to pick them up so he would be able to identify them more easily. He spoke very good English and his name was Javier. "So I was told to first take you to where you will be staying. Is this fine with you?" Javier asked. He was a very polite younger person who appeared to be around 25. He was skinny with a tan skin color and was of medium height. "Yes, that would be fine" said both George and Laura at the same time. So they loaded their bags into the car and started to drive away. Now as they went down the roads they noticed how the roads were set up entirely different than the roads were like back home. They were narrower and there was so many turns and twists in the road. Also, the cars went slower and there was much honking of horns in an attempt to get people to move faster. One thing they learned prior to coming here was that the speed would be in kilometers per hour and not miles per hour. That of course is something that is normal in every other country but the United States. Also, in Costa Rica you never have the right of way as a pedestrian. Their thinking is that since the car is bigger you should have to wait as a pedestrian.

So they finally pulled up to the house were they would be staying about after an hour of riding in the car. They first impressions of the house was that it was rather small but still looked nice. It was surrounded by a gated fence which is normal in Costa Rica to keep potential robbers away. Just about every home is surrounded by some type of fence that requires either a key to open or a remote to electronically open it. So they went through the gate, this one was the electronic type, and they came to a stop right in front of the house. The family they would be staying with came out right about then to greet them. The mother was Maribel, the father was Jose, and their only child, a son, was named Daniel or as he was commonly called, Danny. It was soon discovered during their first introductions and greetings that their English was a bit more broken. So after the greeting was over the family proceeded to help unload the car and show George and Laura to their room. It was a rather small house. Upon entering there was the main living area with a room coming off of it, which was the kitchen, and a hallway that lead back to where the three bedrooms were. There were two bathrooms, one for the master bedroom and one for the two guest bedrooms. The rooms were plain and simple, they were smaller than what is normally found in the United States, and it was a cozy home without all of the extravagant decorations and knickknacks that you typically find in an American home.

As they were unpacking, both George and Laura remarked on how nice of a place they had to stay in. "I really like how the house is plain and small but still has that cozy home feeling" remarked Laura. George on the other hand was just happy that he had a bathroom. "It was not like we were not going to have one" said Laura. "What did you think; we were going to be sleeping on the floor and having to go outside to use the restroom" Laura said jokingly. "No, but you just never know what you are going to run into on trips like this" said George with a smile on his face. So after unpacking they were served a light snack as they had not eaten that much over the course of the day. After eating the snack they were back in the car to head over the church. It would be mostly a private meeting over dinner with the pastor of the church to discuss the upcoming year and their expectations and just what they would be doing. It promised to be a good and exciting year for both George and Laura.

So off they went onto the winding and long roads to the church. It was a long trip due to the road conditions and the amount of traffic present. "Wow, I have never seen this amount of traffic on these roads" remarked the driver in Spanish. What normally would only take them ten minutes ended up taking them twice the amount this time. So they arrived at the church a few minutes later than expected. The church was small and surrounded by a barbed wire fence as was normal in the area. The pastor was outside to greet them when they arrived. "Nice to meet you" he said. The pastor's name was Pastor Renee. He was rather short with black hair. He was middle aged and liked to dress up nicely everyday in dress slacks and a dress shirt. "Nice to meet you too" both George and Laura said with enthusiasm. They were invited inside and they noticed how nice the church was in the inside. It had a large first level area that the chairs were set up for worship and a ramp that went to the classrooms upstairs. The church also had a school where they taught grades 1-12 on an American based curriculum.

After the tour of the building they sat down in his office for the conversation "So, how did the trip go" Pastor Renee asked. This started a conversation on how their trip went coming down. Both

George and Laura remarked that they enjoyed the plane ride and everything went along pretty uneventful. "Okay then how do you plan on adjusting to the culture down here in the upcoming year? Pastor Renee asked. Well this question brought up more thought and deeper thinking in both George and Laura. They had never really given much thought into the culture adjustment they would have to undergo. "Things are different down here" Pastor Renee remarked. "I have been to the United States and found that people up there are so much more close minded. They are not as open to change. I think you will find it a pleasant surprise with the openness of people down here. They will listen to what you have to say. You can go up to a stranger and talk to them about God and they will listen. Whereas back in the United States people might look at you like you are strange or worse yet they will walk away from you and ignore you or they might even make threatening comments back to you. I found this out when I was there. You will like it down here better I think. I don't think there is much of a culture shock but I do think you will find the adjustment to be more pleasant and something that is good for you. George and Laura seemed to be taken aback at this response. It really reassured them for the upcoming year.

So the next question that was asked of both of them was what they would most like to do while they are down here. "What interests you the most?" Pastor Renee asked. "I like to create the most pleasurable and enjoyable experiences for the both of you while you are here. Therefore if I know what you like to do the most I can tailor this whole trip to your likes." This seemed to have surprised both George and Laura for they did not expect their wants and needs to be taken into account here. So George spoke first which is unusual because he is the quiet type that always lets Laura speak first. "I really like to do hands on work" George said with much enthusiasm over being asked what he liked to do. "I really like to do something that involves construction work and something where you can visually see what you have accomplished in the end. So the next one to speak was Laura. "I like to read stories and do small tasks like helping to distribute food to the people. A lot of what I like to do is something that you cannot see visually but it is affecting the people on the inside and spiritually. You distribute food and supplies and they might be quickly consumed so what you end up seeing is someone that has a full stomach and a smile because they did not have to go hungry this evening." Well, both of these things can be done while you are down here" said Pastor Renee. "I see that you both kind of like to do different things so what I would propose is that you both do separate missions in the area." This proposal was quickly accepted by both George and Laura and the conversation and their meeting was quickly coming to a close when Pastor Renee suggested that they both have dinner. So they sat down at a table in the main area of the church and they proceeded to eat their dinner. After dinner they said goodbye for the night and went back to their house where it took much less time to get there this trip. They both remarked on how this was going to be a great year and proceeded straight to bed having both been very tired from the long day.

So the next day dawned on them. They woke up and were greeted by the family at the table for their breakfast meal. It was a nice sunny day. In Costa Rica the sun typically is up by 5:30 AM. This means most people there are early risers and wake up at around 6:00 even on non workdays and weekends. So after waking up and eating breakfast they tried to learn a little Spanish. Typically every morning they would spend some time, maybe an hour, in a little Spanish lesson. This allowed them to quickly become familiar with the language and by halfway through the year they were able to ask many questions and respond to them in Spanish. This is what is known as conversational Spanish. By knowing conversational Spanish they are able to speak in a setting that requires them to know directions or to be able to get to know someone that might not be able to speak English well. However they are not as skilled at reading Spanish. Being able to read Spanish takes more time and practice and they were not as good at that skill yet. So they had a mini lesson in the morning not to mention all of the actual Spanish speaking they heard and participated in throughout the day. So by being surrounded by Spanish speakers and by being in a Spanish speaking environment it was much easier to learn the language in a shorter amount of time.

So after these morning sessions they typically went to the church to spend their day there. Some of the tasks involved building things or construction work. This was more suited to George's likes. Other things involved going out into the community and evangelizing. This kind of activity was much more suited to Laura's likes. So throughout the month of January they learned how to do many of these types of activities. George was kind of shy at evangelizing because he was not the outgoing type. He was a friendly and nice person but to just go up to a complete stranger and talk to them was not his thing. Laura on the other hand was very outgoing and liked to go out and evangelize. Now they did take many classes and worked on Bible studies and they worked on conversation skills. Usually when out evangelizing in the community they had interpreters to make it easier to speak to people that did not speak English that well. So during the classes they took they concentrated on how to relate to people better and how to get them to be closer to God. While out evangelizing they had a normal approach that they would take when talking to someone. They would start out by getting to know that person, and then they would ask them if they have accepeted or know about Christ. Depending on the answer to that question they would either explain to them about God and Christianity or if the person already knew about Christianity and had accepted Christ they would ask them about prayer concerns. After taking any prayer concerns that the person might have they would pray for them. During the prayer they would touch on their prayer concerns and depending on whether the person had accepted Christ or not they would either have the person ask Christ into their hearts or pray that God would continue to work in and through them.

So as the winter turned into spring they continued to do these types of activities. Whether they would be doing community outreaches or participating in construction work they pressed on with much enthusiasm in their hearts and minds. Almost every week they would have a meeting with Pastor Renee to discuss the past week and to take a look at the upcoming week. Concerns and questions were discussed during this time. The couple also attended the church services on Sunday mornings and the youth services Wednesday evenings. They started to like the contemporary worship music as they found it much more uplifting and a more intense form of worship than the traditional hymns. So there were concerns that had to be discussed during these weekly meetings. George was starting to fell homesick and missing his family back home. So they started keeping more in touch with family back home and trying to let them know how things were going down here. That would probably have to be the more pressing issue. Other than that they both thoroughly enjoyed being down here. They often were split up and worked separately in different groups. George's work being more construction related and Laura's being more of the community outreach type. However they both tried all of the different activities.

Laura became gradually better at hands on work and George gradually became better at community outreach and people relations. They were both seeing how they were improving and learning new tools to reach out to God's people.

So the months continued to move on for the year. Spring went well and they continued to do many activities in the area. Summer finally arrived and they found that groups would be arriving from all over the USA to spend a week down there. While there these groups would be doing mostly the same things they were doing just that it would be condensed into the time span of a week. So these groups arrived from local churches all over the USA and were warmly greeted by George and Laura and all of the people at the church. They had much fun together with these groups and they realized how many things could get accomplished with the extra people. They enjoy these groups and make an impact on their lives as well.

After summer things kind of went back to normal. George and Laura quickly realized that this wonderful year was about to come to an end. They had made many memories and they would certainly never forget this for the rest of their lives. It had finally come time to say goodbye at the end of the year and head back home where their family would most certainly have missed them over the course of the year. They gave their hugs and said that they would miss them very much. They also mentioned the possibility of coming back next summer for a week or two to visit. They had packed up and loaded the car and were driven to the airport. They checked their bags in and went to pay their exit tax. In Costa Rica you have to pay an exit tax to leave the country which at the time of this writing in November, 2012 is $26 USD. So after paying this tax they went through security and proceeded to wait for their flight home. It was a pretty uneventful flight and they talked the whole time about their experiences and about what they wanted to share with their church back home. They arrived in Houston and changed planes to head for Pittsburgh. They arrived in Pittsburgh and went to their house in Ohio and unpacked and settled down. George would return to his job the following week as would Laura.

The Sunday they had agreed with Pastor Doug to share their experiences had finally arrived. They got up in front of the church and shared all of what had happened to them in the past year. George said, "I enjoyed seeing how grateful people were when you did things for them. They are just such a loving and kind and friendly type of people." Laura said, "I also enjoyed seeing this. But what hit me the most would have to be this little child that said he had not had a good meal for a week. You could tell by his appearance that he did not eat well. We feed him and his family and he was very thankful for that." So the congregation applauded and George and Laura were glad of their opportunity to share these experiences. Even through these difficulties they had adjusting to a language and everything else they had a most rewarding and adventurous year.

They eventually did return to Costa Rica and got to see all of their old friends again that next summer. It quickly became a tradition that they go there every summer for a week. This continued on for the next ten years until they decided to find other places to go instead. But they never forgot about those people in Costa Rica that they had had so many memories with that year. They continued to help out in the community and the whole trip seemed to spark a further interest in giving back even after they returned. So ends the story of this couple that decided to take a leap out in faith and explore a whole different country. May other people be inspired by this story and continue to make their own impacts in their own way.

The End

16676076R00020

Made in the USA
Charleston, SC
05 January 2013